A BUTTERFLY'S LIFE CYCLE

By George Pendergast

Gareth Stevens
PUBLISHING

Please visit our website, www.garethstevens.com. For a free color catalog of all our high-quality books, call toll free 1-800-542-2595 or fax 1-877-542-2596.

Library of Congress Cataloging-in-Publication Data

Pendergast, George.
A butterfly's life cycle / by George Pendergast.
p. cm. — (Cycles in nature)
Includes index.
ISBN 978-1-4824-1651-0 (pbk.)
ISBN 978-1-4824-1652-7 (6-pack)
ISBN 978-1-4824-1650-3 (library binding)
1. Butterflies — Life cycles — Juvenile literature. I. Title.
QL544.2 P46 2015
595.78—d23

Published in 2016 by
Gareth Stevens Publishing
111 East 14th Street, Suite 349
New York, NY 10003

Copyright © 2016 Gareth Stevens Publishing

Designer: Sarah Liddell
Editor: Ryan Nagelhout

Photo credits: Cover, p. 1 Sari ONeal/Shutterstock.com; p. 5 Lynnya/Shutterstock.com; p. 7 Mau Horng/Shutterstock.com; p. 9 Cathy Keifer/Shutterstock.com; p. 11 Ron Rowan Photography/Shutterstock.com; p. 13 LeAnnMarie/Shutterstock.com; pp. 15, 17, 21 StevenRussellSmithPhotos/Shutterstock.com; p. 19 (background) jajaladdawan/Shutterstock.com; p. 19 (cycle) BlueRingMedia/Shutterstock.com.

Printed in the United States of America

CPSIA compliance information: Batch #CS16GS: For further information contact Gareth Stevens, New York, New York at 1-800-542-2595.

CONTENTS

Boldface words appear in the glossary.

The Monarch

Butterflies live interesting lives. They go through many changes as they get older. This is called a life cycle. Monarch butterflies have one of the most interesting life cycles of any butterfly. Let's learn more about it!

A butterfly starts its life as an egg. Butterflies lay eggs on plant leaves, plant stems, or other objects. If you look closely at an egg, you can see a caterpillar growing inside!

Crawling Caterpillars

The eggs grow for about 4 days. When they **hatch**, caterpillars come out. Caterpillars are butterfly larvae. They eat all the time. They start eating the leaves they hatch on. That's why eggs are laid there!

Caterpillars don't stay caterpillars for very long. They eat as much as they can for about 2 weeks. Monarch caterpillars eat a plant called milkweed. They molt, or shed, their skin, four or more times as they grow bigger.

Inside the Chrysalis

The caterpillar then sticks itself to a stem or leaf and wraps itself in silk it makes. The caterpillar is now a pupa. It stays inside this shell, called a chrysalis (KRIH-suh-lihs) for about 10 days.

Not much happens on the outside during the pupa stage, but the caterpillar is changing inside the chrysalis. The caterpillar is growing into a butterfly! It's growing wings and other organs. This big change is called a **metamorphosis**.

15

All Grown Up

When the butterfly is fully formed, it breaks out of the chrysalis. Its wings are soft and folded at first, but after a few hours, the butterfly can fly!

17

Most monarch butterflies live about 2 to 6 weeks. These butterflies lay eggs in the spring and summer. Butterflies that hatch late in the summer live longer. They live 6 to 8 months. They need to **hibernate** to live through the winter.

The Butterfly Life Cycle

egg
4 days

larva (caterpillar)
about 2 weeks

pupa (in chrysalis)
about 10 days

adult butterfly
2–6 weeks
(some live 6–8 months)

19

Big Travels

Monarch butterflies that come out of their chrysalis in late summer **migrate** south to places like Mexico and California. Many travel up to 2,500 miles (4,023 km). In spring, they come out of hibernation, fly north, and lay eggs again. This keeps the butterfly's life cycle going!

GLOSSARY

hatch: to break open or come out of

hibernate: to be in a sleeplike state for a long period of time, usually during winter

metamorphosis: the process of change that a bug goes through during its life

migrate: to move to a warmer place for the winter

FOR MORE INFORMATION

BOOKS

Guillain, Charlotte. *Life Story of a Butterfly*. Chicago, IL: Capstone Heinemann Library, 2015.

Markovics, Joyce L. *Monarch Butterflies*. New York, NY: Bearport Publishing, 2015.

Stewart, Melissa. *How Does a Caterpillar Become a Butterfly? And Other Questions About Butterflies*. New York, NY: Sterling Children's Books, 2015.

WEBSITES

Growing Up Butterfly
natgeotv.com/ca/great-migrations/videos/ growing-up-butterfly
Watch a butterfly go through its life cycle.

Life Cycle of Butterflies and Moths
kidsbutterfly.org/life-cycle
Learn even more about the four different stages of a butterfly's life cycle.

INDEX